FLORALS
Adult Coloring Book
Calming Art Therapy

Blossom Lore Collection
The Journey of Floral Symbolism and Meanings.

Evie Vincent Publishing

This Book Belongs To

_____

Hello EVP Fans!

Journey into the Florals Coloring Book!

This coloring book provides a unique offering that blends education and artistry. Come in and explore little-known facts and hidden meanings about your favorite blooms while you color each exquisite illustration.

Thank you again for your support, and we hope you continue to find joy and relaxation within the pages of our coloring books.

With Gratitude,
Evie Vincent Publishing

Sunflowers

Adoration and Admiration:

Sunflowers are known for their bright and cheerful appearance, symbolizing adoration, admiration, and loyalty. Giving sunflowers can convey feelings of love, appreciation, and admiration for the recipient.

Daisies

Innocence and Purity:

Daisies are often seen as symbols of innocence and purity due to their simple and delicate appearance. Giving daisies can convey a sense of purity, innocence, and sincerity in relationships.

Ranunculus

Charm and Attraction:

Ranunculus flowers are admired for their vibrant colors and delicate petals, symbolizing charm, attractiveness, and allure. Giving ranunculus can convey feelings of admiration and attraction towards the recipient.

BlueBonnets

Texas Pride:

Bluebonnets are deeply associated with Texas and its cultural identity. Giving bluebonnets as a gift can symbolize pride in one's Texan heritage or appreciation for the state's natural beauty.

Poppies

Remembrance and Memorial:

Poppies are often associated with remembrance, particularly in countries like the United States, Canada, and the United Kingdom, where they are worn on Remembrance Day or Memorial Day to honor soldiers who have died in war. Giving poppies as a gift can symbolize respect, gratitude, and remembrance for the sacrifices made by veterans and fallen heroes.

Peonies

Romance and Love:

Peonies are considered symbols of romance, love, and affection. Giving peonies as a gift can convey deep admiration, love, and devotion to a romantic partner or someone special.

POSIES

Expression of Affection:

Posies have long been associated with expressions of affection and sentimentality. Giving posies as a gift can convey feelings of love, friendship, or appreciation to the recipient.

Peonies

Happiness and Joy:

Peonies are renowned for their lush, luxurious blooms and vibrant colors, symbolizing happiness, joy, and prosperity. Giving peonies as a gift can bring a sense of joy and celebration to the recipient's life, making them ideal for birthdays, anniversaries, or other happy occasions.

Poppy

Hope and Resilience:

Poppies have also been associated with hope and resilience, particularly in the aftermath of war and conflict. Giving poppies as a gift can convey a message of hope for peace, healing, and recovery in the face of adversity.

Pansies

Edible Flowers:

Pansies are edible flowers and are often used to decorate cakes, pastries, and salads. They have a mild, slightly sweet flavor, making them a popular choice for culinary purposes.

PLUMERIA

Fragrant Flowers:

Plumeria flowers are highly fragrant, with a sweet, tropical scent that varies depending on the variety. The fragrance of plumeria flowers is often used in perfumes, lotions, and candles.

HYDRANGEA

Color-Changing Flowers:

The color of hydrangea flowers can change depending on the pH level of the soil. Acidic soil (pH below 7) tends to produce blue flowers, while alkaline soil (pH above 7) results in pink flowers. Neutral soil (pH around 7) typically produces white flowers.

IRIS

Ancient Symbolism:

Irises have been cultivated for thousands of years and hold symbolic significance in various cultures. In ancient Greece, they were associated with the goddess Iris, who personified the rainbow and served as a messenger between gods and humans.

TULIPS

Origin and Symbolism:

Tulips are native to Central Asia and were first cultivated by the Turks in the Ottoman Empire. They became highly prized in Dutch culture during the Dutch Golden Age and are now closely associated with the Netherlands. In Turkish culture, tulips symbolize paradise on Earth.

DAISIES

Ancient Symbolism:

Daisies have been cultivated for centuries and hold symbolic significance in various cultures. In ancient Roman mythology, daisies were associated with innocence and purity and were dedicated to the goddess Venus.

Posies

Medieval Significance:

In medieval Europe, posies were often used for their purported medicinal properties. Different flowers and herbs were chosen for posies based on their believed ability to ward off illness or disease.

PEONIES

Ancient Roots:

Peonies have a long history and have been cultivated for over 2,000 years. They are native to Asia, particularly China, where they have been revered for centuries as symbols of wealth, honor, and beauty.

WILDFLOWERS

Adaptability:

Wildflowers have evolved to thrive in diverse environments, from deserts to mountain meadows and coastal plains. Their adaptability allows them to survive and reproduce in challenging conditions.

WILDFLOWERS

Pollinator Magnet:

Wildflowers are essential for pollinators such as bees, butterflies, and hummingbirds. Their nectar-rich blooms attract pollinators, helping to support healthy ecosystems and biodiversity.

WILDFLOWERS

Native Species:

Many wildflowers are native plants that have been growing in their respective regions for thousands of years. They play a vital role in local ecosystems, providing food and habitat for native wildlife.

WILDFLOWERS

Seed Bombs:

Seed bombs, also known as seed balls or seed grenades, are small balls of clay, compost, and wildflower seeds. They are often used in guerrilla gardening and conservation efforts to restore habitats and beautify urban spaces.

Chrysanthemums

Cultural Significance:

Chrysanthemums hold significant cultural importance in various countries. In Japan, they are the national flower and are celebrated during the annual Festival of Happiness (Kiku Matsuri). Chrysanthemums are also associated with longevity, honor, and joy in Chinese culture.

CALLA LILIES

Symbolism:

Calla lilies have various symbolic meanings in different cultures. In Western cultures, they are often associated with purity, elegance, and rebirth, making them popular choices for weddings and other special occasions. In some Eastern cultures, however, calla lilies are associated with death and are used in funeral arrangements.

STARGAZER LILIES

Signature Scent:

Stargazer lilies are renowned for their powerful and intoxicating fragrance, which is often described as sweet and spicy with hints of floral and citrus notes. The fragrance of Stargazer lilies can fill a room and is prized in floral arrangements and perfumery.

ORCHIDS

Longevity:

Orchids are long-lived plants, with some species capable of surviving for decades or even centuries under the right conditions. With proper care, orchids can continue to bloom year after year, bringing beauty and joy to their owners.

TULIPS

Historical Significance:

Tulips have a rich history dating back to the Ottoman Empire in the 16th century. They were highly prized and became symbols of wealth and status during the Dutch Golden Age. The period even saw a speculative economic bubble known as "Tulip Mania."

Protea

Ancient Origins:

Protea is one of the oldest flowering plant families, with fossil records dating back over 75 million years. They are native to the southern hemisphere, particularly South Africa, Australia, and parts of South America.

BIRDS OF PARADISE

Variety of Species:

There are over 40 species of birds of paradise, each with its own distinct flower shape, color, and size. Some species have elongated, curved flowers resembling bird beaks, while others have flamboyant, fan-shaped blooms.

BLEEDING HEARTS

Botanical Name:

Bleeding hearts belong to the genus Lamprocapnos (formerly Dicentra), which includes several species of herbaceous perennials native to Asia and North America.

BLUEBONNETS

Natural Beauty and Appreciation:

Bluebonnets are admired for their stunning beauty and vibrant blue color. Giving bluebonnets as a gift can convey admiration for the recipient's natural beauty or appreciation for the beauty of nature itself.

PEONIES

Good Fortune and Prosperity:

In some cultures, peonies are believed to symbolize good fortune, prosperity, and happiness. Giving peonies as a gift may convey wishes for abundance, success, and joy in the recipient's life.

POSIES

Environmental Impact:

Posies can have a positive impact on the environment when they include locally sourced, seasonal flowers and foliage. Choosing sustainable options for posies supports local growers and reduces the carbon footprint associated with flower production and transportation.

POPPIES

Dreams and Imagination:

In mythology and folklore, poppies have been associated with sleep, dreams, and the imagination. Giving poppies as a gift may symbolize wishes for peaceful rest, sweet dreams, and creative inspiration.

PEONIES

Beauty and Elegance:

Peonies are admired for their stunning beauty, graceful appearance, and luxurious blooms. Giving peonies as a gift can express admiration for someone's beauty, grace, and elegance, both in physical appearance and character.

Poppies

Resilience:

Poppies are resilient flowers that can thrive in harsh conditions and symbolize resilience, strength, and endurance. Giving poppies as a gift may convey a message of support, encouragement, and admiration for someone facing challenges or adversity.

PEONIES

Sustainability:

Peonies are generally low-maintenance plants that require minimal inputs once established. They are drought-tolerant and deer-resistant, making them suitable for sustainable landscaping and garden designs.

Poppy

Color Variations:

While red poppies are the most commonly recognized, poppies come in a variety of colors, including pink, orange, yellow, white, and purple. Some species, such as Papaver rhoeas, produce bi-colored or multi-colored blooms with contrasting markings and patterns.

POPPIES

Cultural Significance:

Poppies have cultural significance in various societies and have been featured in art, literature, and folklore for centuries. They are often associated with remembrance, sleep, and death, and have been used as symbols in ceremonies, rituals, and memorials.

ROSES

Symbolism:

Roses have been symbols of love, romance, and beauty in various cultures and traditions throughout history. Different rose colors carry different symbolic meanings, with red roses symbolizing love and passion, white roses symbolizing purity and innocence, and yellow roses symbolizing friendship and joy, among others.

RANUNCULUS

Tuberous Roots:

Ranunculus plants grow from tuberous roots, which store nutrients and moisture to support the plant's growth and flowering. These roots can be dug up and divided to propagate new plants, making ranunculus a popular choice for gardeners and florists

HIBISCUS

Edible Flowers:

Many hibiscus species produce edible flowers that are used in culinary applications. Hibiscus flowers can be dried and brewed into herbal tea, which is known for its tart, cranberry-like flavor and vibrant red color.

SUNFLOWERS

Native to the Americas:

Sunflowers are native to the Americas, with their wild ancestors originating in North America. They were domesticated by indigenous peoples thousands of years ago and cultivated for their seeds, oil, and ornamental value.

PANSIES

Pollinator Attraction:

Pansies are attractive to pollinators such as bees and butterflies, making them beneficial for garden ecosystems. By planting pansies, gardeners can support pollinator populations and promote biodiversity in their gardens.

IRIS

Species Diversity:

The genus Iris is incredibly diverse, consisting of hundreds of species and thousands of cultivated varieties. This diversity includes tall bearded irises, miniature dwarf irises, Siberian irises, Japanese irises, and many more, each with its own unique characteristics and growing requirements.

HYDRANGEA

Symbol of Abundance:

In some cultures, hydrangeas are considered symbols of abundance, wealth, and prosperity. They are often used in floral arrangements for weddings, celebrations, and other auspicious occasions.

PLUMERIA

Drought Tolerance:

Plumeria trees are drought-tolerant once established and prefer well-drained soil. They are well-suited to dry, tropical climates and can thrive with minimal water once their root systems are established.

Chrysanthemums

Modern Uses:

Beyond their traditional symbolism and cultural significance, chrysanthemums are also used in modern scientific research. Extracts from chrysanthemum flowers have been studied for their potential medicinal properties, including anti-inflammatory, antimicrobial, and antioxidant effects.

CALLA LILIES

Container Plants:

Calla lilies can be grown in containers, making them suitable for patio gardens, balconies, and indoor spaces. They prefer well-drained soil and bright, indirect sunlight. Container-grown calla lilies can be brought indoors during cold weather or overwintered in a protected location.

Stargazer Lilies

Cultural Significance:

Stargazer lilies have been featured prominently in art, literature, and popular culture. They have been depicted in paintings, films, and television shows, and their distinctive appearance and fragrance have made them enduring symbols of beauty and elegance.

Be Uniquely You

We hope you enjoyed the Florals Collection.

Visit us at www.EvieVincentPublishing.com to view our offerings--Sea Life, Botanicals, and Beachfront Adult Coloring Book under our Calming Art Therapy Collections.

Stay true to yourself and live abundantly.
Evie Vincent Publishing

References and Sources

Catherine Boeckmann. (2022, February 2). Flower Meanings: The Language of Flowers. Old Farmer's Almanac. https://www.almanac.com/flower-meanings-language-flowers

Language of flowers. (2021, January 27). Wikipedia. https://en.wikipedia.org/wiki/Language_of_flowers

www.ingramcontent.com/pod-product-compliance
Lightning Source LLC
Chambersburg PA
CBHW081016040426
42444CB00014B/3228